# Ocean Wonders

# KINGFISHER

First published 2016 by Kingfisher
an imprint of Macmillan Children's Books
20 New Wharf Road, London N1 9RR
Associated companies throughout the world
www.panmacmillan.com

Copyright © Macmillan Publishers International Ltd 2016

Interior design by Tall Tree Ltd
Cover design by Peter Clayman

Adapted from an original text by Margaret Hynes

ISBN 978-0-7534-3977-7

A CIP catalogue record for this book is available from the British Library.

Printed in China

9 8 7 6 5 4 3 2 1
1TR/0516/WKT/UG/128MA

Picture credits
The Publisher would like to thank the following for permission to reproduce their material.
Top = t; Bottom = b; Centre = c; Left = l; Right = r
Front cover: Shutterstock/Claude Huot; Back cover iStock/Jan Will; Pages-1 Shutterstock/Rich Carey; 2–3 Corbis/
Martin Harvey; 4–5b Superstock/Cusp; 4br FLPA/Reinhard Dirscherl; 5cl NaturePL/Jose B. Ruiz; 5r Natural
History Picture Agency (NHPA)/Michael Patrick O'Neill; 5cr Seapics/Ross Armstrong; 5bl Seapics/Ross
Armstrong; 5b Seapics/Ross Armstrong; 8–9ct Corbis/Nic Bothma; 8–9c Corbis/Nic Bothma; 9br Getty/Philippe
Huguen/AFP; 11b Photoshot/AllCanada Photos; 12c SPL/M.I. Walker; 12–13 Shutterstock/Peter J Kovacs;
13cr NaturePL/David Shale; 14tr Shutterstock/nice_pictures; 14cr Alamy/WILDLIFE GmbH; 14cl; Alamy/
WILDLIFE GmbH; 16bl Shutterstock/Luis Chavier; 16c Shutterstock/ivvv1975; 16cr Shutterstock/Olga
Khoroshunova; 16br Shutterstock/Rui Gomes; 16–17 Shutterstock/John A. Anderson; 17cr Shutterstock/Milena
Katzer; 17b Shutterstock/Rich Carey; 18tl Seapics/Robert L. Pitman; 21bl Shutterstock/Richard Whitcombe;
22–23 Getty/National Geographic Society; 22b Shutterstock/Rich Carey; 23bl SPL/Alexis Rosenfeld; 24bl Getty/
Terence Spencer/Time & Life Pictures; 24–25 Alamy/Poelzer; 25c Corbis/Ralph White; 26b Corbis/Martin
Harvey; 26–27 Shutterstock/Photofish; 27tr Alamy/Images & Stories; 27c Corbis/Akhtar Soomro/epa;
28bl Alamy/EricNathan; 28–29 Alamy/All Canada Photos/Wayne Lynch.

# Contents

# Ocean life

Oceans and seas are home to a wide range of living things. Plants are found only in the sunlit parts of the ocean near the surface. Animals live at all depths. Down on the seabed a single rock can be home to as many as ten major groups of animals, such as corals, molluscs and sponges.

## Mammals

All **mammals** need air to breathe, so you might be surprised to find mammals living in the sea. There are many sea mammals, however, and these include dolphins, sea lions, walruses, whales, porpoises and manatees. They all come up to the surface to breathe air and they give birth to live young.

## Echinoderms

Starfish, sea urchins and sea cucumbers are all echinoderms. This group of spiny-skinned animals contains about 6000 species and they are found only in the oceans. Echinoderms are simple animals – they do not even have a brain!

## Fish

Fish are the most diverse group of animals in the oceans. There are more than 15,300 known species of ocean fish and scientists believe that there are thousands more to be discovered.

## Ocean forests

Forests of giant seaweeds, called kelp, provide a home for many different creatures in the shallow, cool waters above rocky seabeds. The tall kelps hold on to the rocky bottom with root-like structures called holdfasts.

### mollusc

An animal with a soft body, no spine and often with a shell. Snails, oysters and squid are molluscs.

## Crustaceans

Crustaceans have a hard skeleton on the outside of their body. They include crabs, shrimp, lobsters and barnacles. Crabs and shrimp can swim, but lobsters can only scuttle along the seabed. Barnacles stick to a hard spot and never move.

## TOP FIVE BITESIZE FACTS

- New marine species are being recorded at an average rate of three per week.

- Kelp can grow up to 60 centimetres a day.

- The biggest lobsters can weigh up to 20 kilograms.

- The largest crab is the Japanese spider crab which can have a leg span of nearly four metres.

- Sailfish can swim at 110 kilometres per hour.

5

# The ocean floor

The ocean floor is a world of great plains, huge mountains, active volcanoes and deep chasms, called trenches. Many of these are formed by the movement of the **tectonic plates** that make up the **Earth's crust**.

A chain of volcanic islands forms where tectonic plates meet.

An island is formed when the summit of a volcano rises above the surface of the water.

Deep trenches occur where two plates push against each other and one slides under the other.

## Beneath the surface

Much of the ocean floor is a flat plain, covered with thick, muddy ooze. Chains of underwater mountains are found beneath the oceans. Hot **magma** bubbles up and cools to form new sea floor as tectonic plates move away on either side. Trenches are formed in subduction zones where the plates collide. Here, volcanoes burst up to create underwater mountains, and some reach the surface as volcanic islands.

### subduction zone
An area where one tectonic plate is diving beneath another into the interior of the Earth.

Hot, soft **mantle** swirls around, carrying plates of the crust.

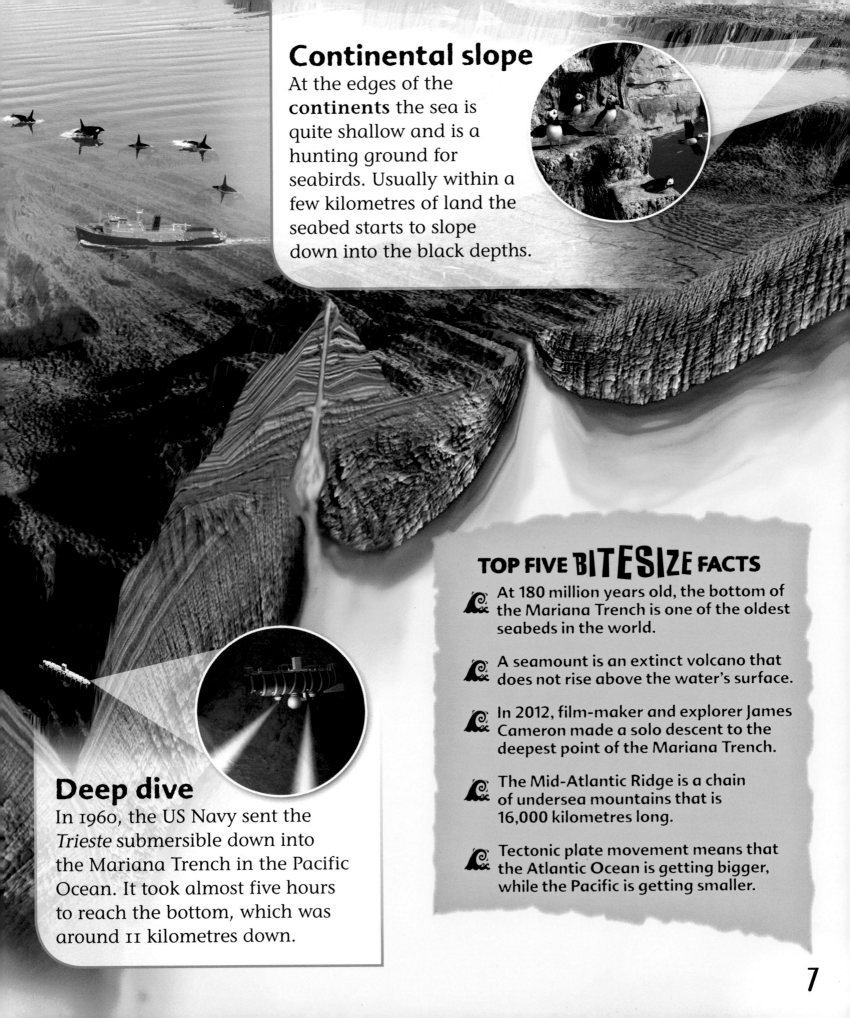

## Continental slope

At the edges of the **continents** the sea is quite shallow and is a hunting ground for seabirds. Usually within a few kilometres of land the seabed starts to slope down into the black depths.

## Deep dive

In 1960, the US Navy sent the *Trieste* submersible down into the Mariana Trench in the Pacific Ocean. It took almost five hours to reach the bottom, which was around 11 kilometres down.

## TOP FIVE BITESIZE FACTS

At 180 million years old, the bottom of the Mariana Trench is one of the oldest seabeds in the world.

A seamount is an extinct volcano that does not rise above the water's surface.

In 2012, film-maker and explorer James Cameron made a solo descent to the deepest point of the Mariana Trench.

The Mid-Atlantic Ridge is a chain of undersea mountains that is 16,000 kilometres long.

Tectonic plate movement means that the Atlantic Ocean is getting bigger, while the Pacific is getting smaller.

7

# All about waves

Ocean waves are ripples of energy. Most waves are caused by winds as they brush against the top of the sea and transfer energy from the air to the water. Waves move this energy across the ocean, pushed in the direction of the wind.

direction of wave movement

The crest is the high point of the wave.

The crest topples forwards and breaks on the beach.

The trough is the low point of the wave.

The wave gets higher as the seabed rises.

The water in each wave moves in circles.

## Making waves

Each wave lifts water particles round in circles, creating crests and troughs on the surface. As waves approach a shore, the movement of the water at the bottom of the wave is slowed by the seabed and the top of the wave spills over.

## epicentre

The point on the Earth's surface directly above the focus of an earthquake.

## TOP FIVE BITESIZE FACTS

- The tallest wave measured 500 metres high in Lituya Bay, Alaska, USA.

- Tsunamis can travel at more than 640 kilometres per hour.

- An early warning system for tsunamis is made up of a network of floating buoys, which send signals to satellites.

- At least 230,000 people were killed by the Indian Ocean tsunami in 2004.

- The 2004 tsunami was caused by the third-largest earthquake recorded.

## Tsunamis

Sometimes reaching heights of 40 metres or more, tsunamis are very destructive waves. They are caused by underwater earthquakes, volcanoes or landslides. The larger the disturbance, the larger and more dangerous the tsunami is.

Water is suddenly lifted.

The ocean plate is pushed below the other plate.

earthquake epicentre

## Storm waves

On calm days, waves barely move, but in storms they move faster and grow higher. These storm waves often cause huge damage.

Waves pound the coastline in southern England.

9

# Water on the move

As the Moon **orbits** the Earth, its **gravity** pulls at the Earth's oceans, causing a bulge in the water that we call high tide. Another bulge forms on the opposite side of the world, creating an area of low tide in-between. The tides change as the bulges of water follow the Moon's orbit.

## Rockpool ecosystem

When the tide goes out from a rocky coast, pools of water are left behind in hollows in the rocks. Each pool is a tiny ecosystem. Limpets and winkles feed on seaweed. Crabs munch on shellfish and **shannies** nibble barnacles and green seaweed. Life in the rockpool is hard. The wildlife must be able to cope with big changes in the water, salt, oxygen and temperature levels in the pool.

**Key**

1 Shore crab

2 Mussels

3 Barnacles

4 Hermit crab

5 Common starfish

6 Sea anemone

7 Shanny (a fish)

**ecosystem**
A community of living things that exist together in the same place.

## High or dry

The sea comes high up on the beach, and then goes back again every day. In some places the difference is huge, with the deep water at high tide allowing sailing boats in and out of a harbour. But at low tide, the water is so shallow that boats either become stuck or they are unable to reach the harbour.

## TOP FIVE BITESIZE FACTS

- Some rivers flowing into the sea also have tides. These are called tidal rivers.

- The greatest difference between low and high tide is more than 16 metres at the Bay of Fundy in Canada.

- Tides are so powerful that they can drive turbines that generate electricity.

- The pull of the Sun's gravity also affects the size of the tides.

- When the Moon and Sun are aligned, their combined gravity causes very high tides called spring tides.

# Layers of life

Scientists divide the oceans into layers, or zones. The light fades as you go deeper. The water also gets colder and the **water pressure** increases with the added weight of the water above.

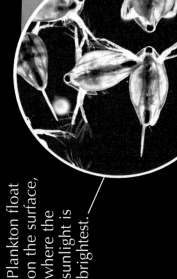

Plankton float on the surface, where the sunlight is brightest.

## Sunlit zone

This zone stretches from the surface to 200 metres below sea level. Here, there is enough light for sea plants and algae to make food. These attract animals who feed on them, and they attract predators, such as tuna and turtles.

## Twilight zone

Beneath the sunlit zone and down to 1000 metres lies the twilight zone. There is just enough light to hunt by, but not enough for sea plants to make food.

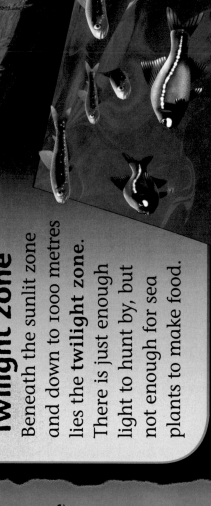

## TOP FIVE BITE|S|ZE FACTS

🐟 Most dark zone fish have gaping mouths to catch what little food there is.

🐟 The deepest recorded fish was a sea ghost snailfish which was spotted at 8,143 metres below the surface.

🐟 More than 90 per cent of all ocean life lives in the sunlit zone.

🐟 Many sea creatures stay in one zone all their life.

🐟 At depths of 200 metres, water pressure is 20 times greater than at the surface.

## Dark zone

Beyond 1000 metres deep is the dark zone. Food is scarce here and the animals rely on what little drifts down from above. The only light in this zone is bioluminescent light, which is produced by some of the animals to lure prey or confuse predators.

A sea spider's stilt-like legs help it to walk on the ocean floor. This creature lives at depths of up to 7400 metres.

**bioluminescent light**
A light given off by some animals to startle predators or to attract prey.

**blubber**
A layer of body fat, up to 30 centimetres thick, that sea mammals use to keep warm.

As the whale bursts upwards, the front flippers make its body spin, while the final push comes from the horizontal fluke, or tail.

## Tracking
Every humpback has unique tail markings. The whales often show their fluke (tail), so scientists use these markings to identify individual whales. This helps to track humpbacks when they migrate.

# Giants of the ocean

Weighing up to 40 tonnes each, humpback whales are famous for their long **migrations**, and for their amazing underwater songs. They are also acrobats, bursting through the surface of the ocean and landing in one of the biggest splashes in the animal world.

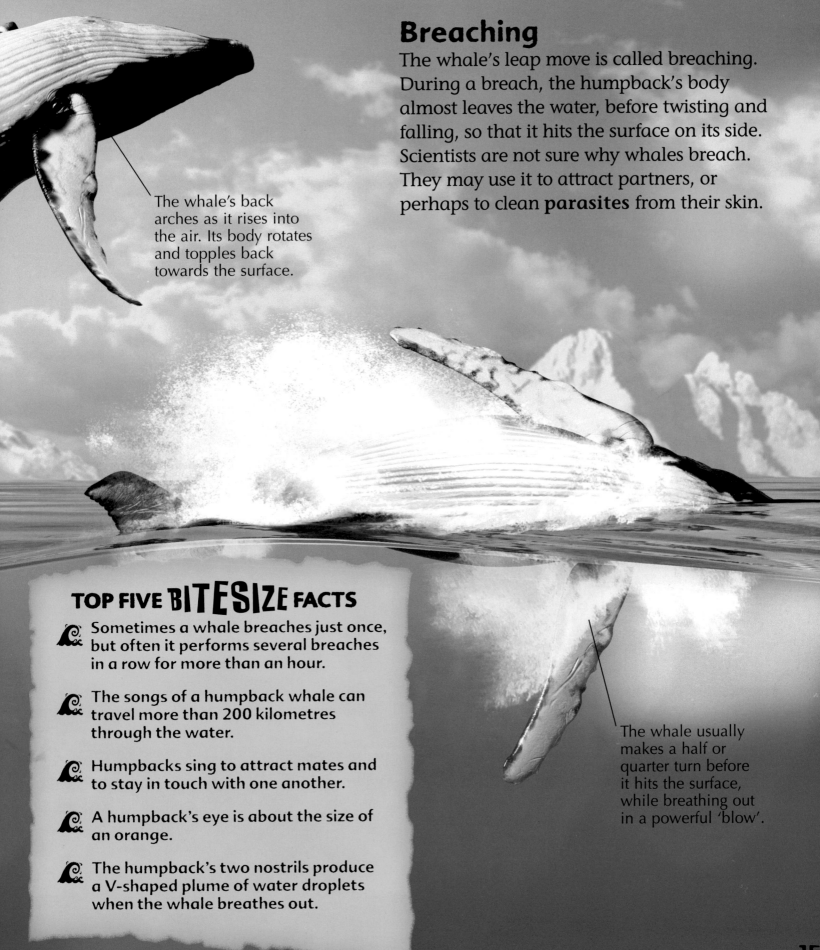

# Breaching

The whale's leap move is called breaching. During a breach, the humpback's body almost leaves the water, before twisting and falling, so that it hits the surface on its side. Scientists are not sure why whales breach. They may use it to attract partners, or perhaps to clean **parasites** from their skin.

The whale's back arches as it rises into the air. Its body rotates and topples back towards the surface.

The whale usually makes a half or quarter turn before it hits the surface, while breathing out in a powerful 'blow'.

## TOP FIVE BITESIZE FACTS

- Sometimes a whale breaches just once, but often it performs several breaches in a row for more than an hour.

- The songs of a humpback whale can travel more than 200 kilometres through the water.

- Humpbacks sing to attract mates and to stay in touch with one another.

- A humpback's eye is about the size of an orange.

- The humpback's two nostrils produce a V-shaped plume of water droplets when the whale breathes out.

# Underwater gardens

Coral reefs are solid structures that are built up from the remains of marine animals called coral polyps. They are found in warm, shallow seas. Reefs grow slowly as the animals that form them multiply, spread and die, adding their skeletons to the reef. Some islands are made entirely of coral.

1

### coral polyp
A tiny creature whose hard skeleton is used to create a coral reef.

## Prickly predator
A hungry crown-of-thorns starfish climbs up on coral and pulls its stomach out of its mouth and over its prey. The starfish releases juices that dissolve the coral, then the starfish's stomach absorbs the **nutrients**.

4

2

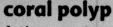
3

5

# Reefs in danger

A healthy reef bursts with life and colour in much the same way as a rainforest does on land. Even the smallest reefs are teeming with hundreds of different types of corals, fish, crabs, starfish, sea urchins and other animals. Sadly, reefs are under threat from human activity. They are broken up for building materials and tourist souvenirs, damaged by divers and suffer from the effects of coastal pollution.

## TOP FIVE BITESIZE FACTS

- Some of today's coral reefs have been growing for 50 million years.

- Coral reefs cover less than one per cent of the ocean floor.

- The most venomous fish, the stonefish, lives in reefs, camouflaged as a stone.

- Plants that grow on coral reefs can be important sources of medicines.

- Scientists believe that threats to coral reefs could mean 30 per cent of them will die in the next 30 years.

**Key**

1  Powder blue tang

2  Clownfish

3  Giant sea anemone

4  Crown-of-thorns starfish

5  Yellow cube boxfish

6  Lionfish

7  Queen angelfish

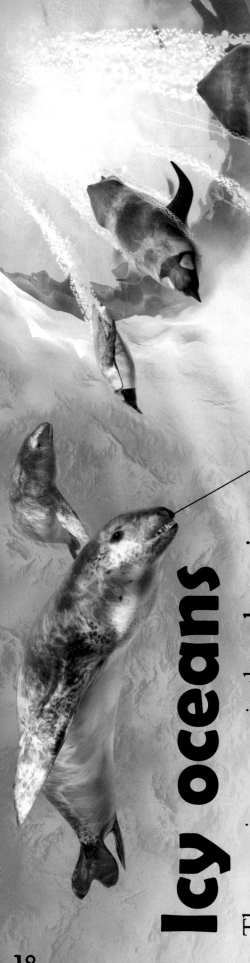

# Icy oceans

There are icy oceans in the polar regions at opposite ends of the globe. The Arctic Ocean in the north is almost completely surrounded by North America, Eurasia and Greenland. In the south, the Southern Ocean surrounds the Antarctic continent. The Southern Ocean is coldest, with surface temperatures ranging between minus 2°C and 2°C. It is also richer in animal life.

## Southern life

Temperatures in the Southern Ocean are influenced by icy winds that blow down from the highlands on Antarctica. In winter, pack ice covers more than half of this ocean and air temperatures drop to between minus 20°C and minus 30°C. Animals such as sponges, anemones, crabs and starfish live on the seabed away from the icy winds. When the ice retreats in summer, birds, seals, whales, fish and squid arrive to hunt for food.

Seals have a thick layer of blubber under their skin to keep them warm.

## Emperor of Antarctica

The emperor penguin is the largest penguin species. Like all penguins, it cannot fly. Instead, it has a **streamlined** body and wings that are adapted for gliding through the water.

🐟 Narwhals are medium-sized whales with one long tusk that can measure three metres long.

🐟 Emperor penguins can stay underwater for 18 minutes, diving down to depths of 535 metres to catch fish and krill.

🐟 The Arctic Ocean is the smallest of the Earth's five oceans.

🐟 In 1958, the submarine USS *Nautilus* became the first vessel to sail beneath the Arctic ice.

🐟 The Arctic ice holds 10 per cent of the world's freshwater.

### pack ice
A floating jigsaw of pieces of ice that drifts freely.

Borch live under the pack ice. These fish are adapted to freezing temperatures.

Red starfish live only in very cold waters, where they feed on dead fish, sponges and other starfish.

The Antarctic anemone uses its long tentacles to catch starfish, sea urchins and jellyfish much larger than itself.

The body of the Antarctic icefish contains special blood that can withstand the freezing temperatures.

19

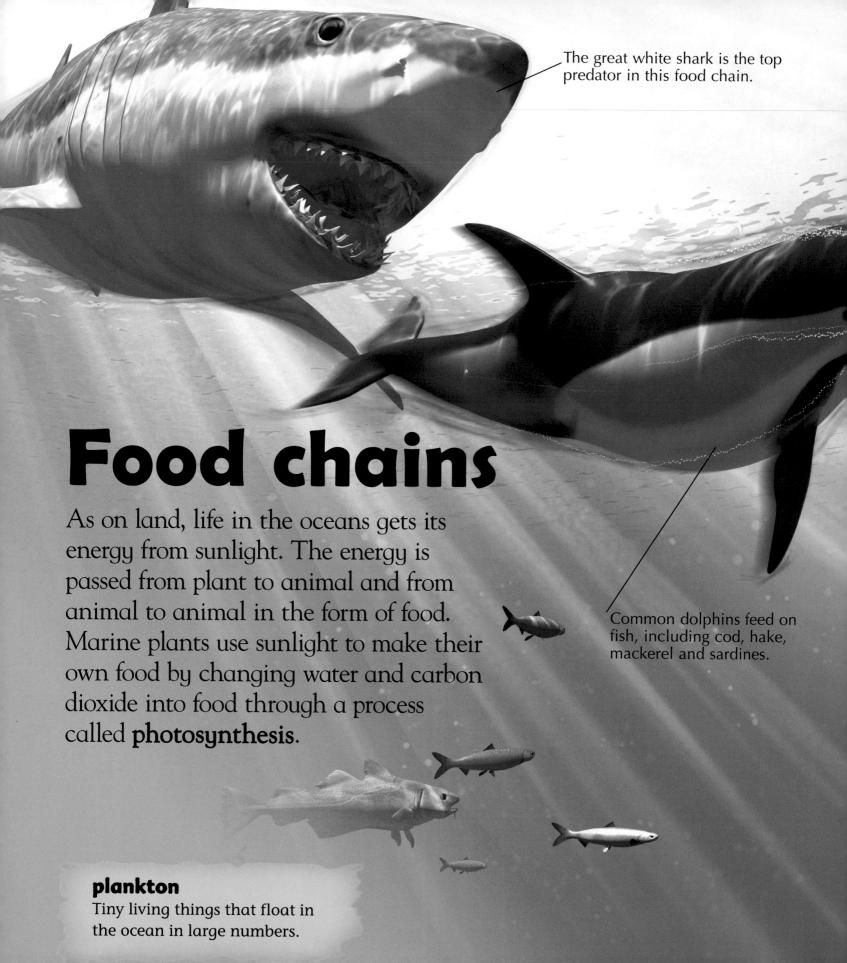

The great white shark is the top predator in this food chain.

# Food chains

As on land, life in the oceans gets its energy from sunlight. The energy is passed from plant to animal and from animal to animal in the form of food. Marine plants use sunlight to make their own food by changing water and carbon dioxide into food through a process called **photosynthesis**.

Common dolphins feed on fish, including cod, hake, mackerel and sardines.

**plankton**
Tiny living things that float in the ocean in large numbers.

# From plant to animal

Much of the ocean's plant life consists of tiny floating plant plankton, or **phytoplankton**. Animal plankton, or **zooplankton**, feed on the phytoplankton. The zooplankton are eaten by small fish, which are in turn food for larger predators. This is a food chain.

Herring eat zooplankton.

Krill are a shrimp-like zooplankton.

Cod eat many different types of sea creatures including herring.

Phytoplankton produce food using sunlight.

# Perfect partners

Not all living things eat each other and some live closely together. Clownfish are **immune** to the sting on a sea anemone's tentacles and so live within the tentacles, safe from predators. In return, the clownfish clean the anemone by eating **debris**.

## TOP FIVE BITESIZE FACTS

- The largest fish in the world, the whale shark, feeds on the smallest creatures. It filters huge amounts of plankton.

- When creatures die, scavengers feed on the bodies, recycling their nutrients.

- All living things in the food chain play a vital role. For example, sharks keep squid populations under control.

- When oil spills or **overfishing** harm a species, they also harm the animals who need that species for food.

- Phytoplankton are called producers because they make food using sunlight.

**submersible**
A small vessel that is
designed to go underwater.

# Underwater explorers

Today's ocean explorers make voyages
of discovery deep below the ocean's
surface rather than across it. They use
deep-diving craft and suits that can
withstand the huge water pressure of
the deep ocean. Some modern ocean
explorers seek out previously
undiscovered forms
of life.

## Mini submarine

Manned submersibles
are like small submarines.
The people on board are
protected from the deep-
ocean pressure inside a
strong capsule. A jointed
arm, controlled from inside
the vessel, allows the crew to
grip and pick up items.

## Mother ship

While submarines and submersibles explore the deep, surface ships are still needed to get close to the investigation site. Once at sea, the surface ship is busy as a research station with laboratories and control centres. It is also home for scientists, engineers, sailors and support staff, such as cooks. Sometimes these people spend months at a time at sea.

## Newt suit

A deep-sea pressure suit is a bit like a personal submarine. The pressure inside the hard shell of such suits is the same as that at the surface. Drager Newt suits, like this one, have fluid-filled joints that allow the divers to move about. Newt suits can be used at depths of 365 metres.

## TOP FIVE BITESIZE FACTS

- Humans have explored less than five per cent of the Earth's oceans.

- Hydrothermal vents are cracks in the seabed through which super-hot water erupts at temperatures of 450°C.

- The deepest a person has dived wearing scuba (self-contained underwater breathing apparatus) gear is 332 metres.

- The deepest free dive without oxygen is 214 metres.

- Submersibles can carry a crew or they can be robotic and controlled from the surface.

# Shipwrecks and treasure

The sea can preserve shipwrecks and **artefacts** by burying them under a layer of mud. These wrecks and artefacts are a valuable source of information for marine archaeologists. These archaeologists make detailed studies of sites, mapping the area and recording each find.

A diver examines the remains of a Roman ship in the Red Sea.

## Wreck preservation

Wooden shipwrecks are often best left where they are. If they are recovered, they need to be sprayed with a waxy solution that stops them drying out. The *Mary Rose* warship, which sank in 1545, is preserved in this way in a museum in Portsmouth, UK.

**marine archaeologist**
A scientist who studies the past by looking at any underwater remains.

## *Titanic*

In 1912, the passenger ship *Titanic* hit an iceberg and sank, killing 1517 people. The wreck was located four kilometres down on the seabed in 1985 by Dr Robert Ballard. A French team used a submersible, *Nautile*, to remove items from the wreck in 1987. This made many people angry. They thought the wreck should be respected as an underwater grave.

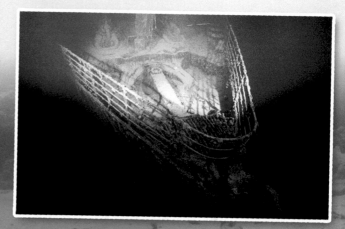

## TOP FIVE BITESIZE FACTS

- The *Vasa* was a Swedish warship that sank in 1628.

- Like the *Mary Rose*, the remains of the *Vasa* were raised in 1961 and preserved in a museum in Stockholm, Sweden.

- Human remains from the *Mary Rose* were found to be archers. We know this because they had strong back and arm muscles from drawing their bows.

- Marine archaeologists use a long thick hose to suck up dirt from a site.

- Marine archaeologists examine the remains of sunken cities.

# Oceans in trouble

Over the years, people have harmed the oceans and they are now in trouble. Overfishing has reduced fish numbers in many places. The oceans are also being poisoned by **pollution** and oil spilled from tankers. Litter has also made its way into the oceans and coral reefs are being destroyed.

Oily seabirds can be cleaned with water and detergent.

## Sinking ship

When a tanker runs aground, every effort is made to remove the oil on board before it spills out. In 2003, the tanker *Tasman Spirit* ran aground near Karachi, Pakistan. About 32,000 tonnes of the 67,000-tonne cargo of oil was transferred to other vessels before the tanker broke in two. The remaining oil leaked out and caused a spill that covered local beaches.

## Oil spills

Huge amounts of oil are transported at sea by tankers, which can be 460 metres long. Sometimes they run aground and spill their oil, causing huge amounts of damage. If seabirds and sea mammals are covered in oil, they often die of the cold because their clogged feathers or fur no longer contain pockets of air to keep them warm. Animals can also die from eating the oil as they try to clean themselves.

**tanker**
A large ship that is designed to carry huge amounts of liquids or gases, such as oil.

# Under threat

The Mediterranean monk seal is one of the world's most endangered marine mammals. Fewer than 700 survive today. Sometimes they are killed accidentally when they become tangled in fishing nets and drown. Other times they are killed deliberately by fishermen, who consider them pests that steal their fish and damage their nets.

The *Tasman Spirit* sinking in the Arabian Sea off Pakistan.

# Oil slick

**Crude oil** is thick, sticky and poisonous. If it leaks from a tanker, it floats on the surface of the water, forming a slick. This covers everything it touches. Slicks have been known to wash up on beaches hundreds of kilometres from the spill site.

## TOP FIVE BITESIZE FACTS

- In 1991, during the First Gulf War, Iraqi forces released nearly one billion litres of oil into the Persian Gulf.

- In 1989, an oil spill from the *Exxon Valdez* tanker covered 28,000 square kilometres, an area larger than Wales.

- The *Exxon Valdez* spill killed up to 250,000 sea birds, 300 seals, 247 bald eagles and 22 orcas.

- Some oil remains on the Alaskan coast, nearly 30 years after the *Exxon Valdez* spill.

- Pollution in the oceans creates 'dead zones' where nothing can live.

27

# The future

Many scientists believe that modern air pollution is warming up the planet faster than usual through a process called the greenhouse effect. This change in the world's **climate** may be affecting the oceans, leading to a rise in sea levels and more frequent and more violent ocean storms.

**ice floe**
A flat, floating chunk of sea ice that is less than 10 kilometres across.

## Melting ice

Most of the Earth's ice is on land, on Greenland and Antarctica. Increasing temperatures may be melting the ice more quickly than usual, causing more water to run into the sea. This raises sea levels and causes flooding in areas near to coasts. The melting is also destroying polar **habitats**. Polar bears must now swim farther to find food because the ice floes from which they feed are melting, becoming smaller and drifting apart.

We can all do things to help reduce greenhouse gases, for example by walking or cycling to work or school.

# Carbon dioxide

The gas carbon dioxide is produced by burning **fossil fuels** in car engines, in central heating and in power plants. The extra carbon dioxide in the **atmosphere** makes the greenhouse effect stronger, possibly causing **global warming**.

## TOP FIVE BITESIZE FACTS

- There is 25 per cent more carbon dioxide in the atmosphere than there was 150 years ago.

- Measurements show that the Earth's average surface temperature is 0.87°C higher than 50 years ago.

- Scientists predict that the Earth's climate will become about 2.5°C warmer during the 21st century.

- Sea levels have risen by 3.5 millimetres a year since 1990.

- By 2100, sea levels will have risen by two metres, submerging low-lying island countries such as the Maldives.

# Glossary

**algae**
Simple, plant-like living things that make their own food using the energy of sunlight.

**artefact**
Objects of important historical interest, such as those found in sunken ships.

**atmosphere**
Layers of gases that surround the Earth.

**climate**
The average weather in a region.

**continent**
One of seven large sheets of rock that rise above the oceans as dry land.

**crude oil**
Thick, raw oil found inside the Earth. It is refined to make petroleum.

**debris**
Dead animal or plant matter eaten by other animals. 'Marine debris' can also refer to human-made rubbish in the oceans that often washes ashore.

**Earth's crust**
The rocky outer shell of the Earth, which is divided into large plates.

**fossil fuels**
Coal, oil and gas made over millions of years from the remains of long-dead plants and other living things.

**global warming**
The gradual warming of the Earth's climate. It may be caused by pollution in the planet's atmosphere.

**gravity**
The invisible pulling force between objects with mass, such as the attraction of the Earth and the Moon, which pull towards one another.

**habitat**
A place where an animal or plant lives.

**immune**
A natural defence against an infection or venom (poison).

**magma**
Hot, runny rock that lies below the Earth's surface. Once magma reaches the surface, it is called lava.

**mammal**
A warm-blooded animal that produces milk for its young.

**mantle**
The thick layer of hot rock between the Earth's crust and its core.

## migration
A very long journey made by some animals to look for food or a place to have their young.

## nutrient
A nourishing chemical in food that a living thing needs to survive.

## orbit
To travel in space around a planet or object. The Moon orbits the Earth.

## overfishing
To take out large numbers of fish from an area of the ocean at a faster rate than the fish can reproduce.

## parasite
An organism that lives in or on another. The relationship helps the parasite but is harmful to the host.

## photosynthesis
The chemical process by which plants and algae use sunlight to change carbon dioxide into food.

## phytoplankton
Very tiny floating water plants that make their own food through photosynthesis. Phytoplankton are a kind of plankton.

## polar regions
Areas around the North and South Poles.

## pollution
The presence of harmful or poisonous things in the environment, for example plastic rubbish in the oceans.

## predator
An animal that catches and feeds on other animals.

## shanny
A long, slender fish with a spiny fin along its back. Also known as a prickleback.

## streamlined
Having a smooth outline that slips easily through water or air.

## tectonic plate
A giant slab of the Earth's crust that moves slowly over the hot, rocky mantle.

## twilight zone
The part of the ocean where there is faint blue light. It sits between the sunlit zone and the dark zone.

## water pressure
The pressure applied to part of a column of water. It is caused by the weight of the water above it.

## zooplankton
Tiny animals that drift in the oceans. Zooplankton are a kind of plankton.

# Index